365

BUSINESS

PRINCIPLES

(A QUICK REMINDER FOR EVERY ENTREPRENEUR
FROM MY 20 FAVOURITE FILMS)

BY

MYRAH DUCKWORTH

SUCCESS COACH

Dedicated to:

Harry Bhanga

Of Arana Ltd (Coventry)

for the best business advice ever.

Reece Turner

and

Josh Dykes

of Speakup (Birmingham)

for

providing me with an audience to share my truths.

Mark Clarke

for

loving me enough to come back.

Foreword:

Josh Dykes

At SPEAKup we've helped thousands of people learn new skills. On the way we've had a lot of ups and downs; it can be tough to keep on track at times, especially when we start having to solve problems in multiple areas.

This book is ideal for anyone who feels the stresses of being busy and working hard. You can literally turn to any page for a nugget of knowledge that will allow you to refocus and keep going in the right direction.

Josh Dykes

SPEAKup Challenge

Head of Operations

http://www.speakupchallenge.com/

Foreword:

Davinder Bahia

This wonderful book is filled with powerful ways to move forward and cast aside doubts and negativity that can hold back progress in your life. Myrah has presented inspiration in a unique and novel way that can be used time and time again for any area of life. As a business owner and manager for over 10 years survival and perseverance have been down to continually finding the fight to go on and this book will help me to feel motivated and feed my drive to succeed.

Davinder Bahia

Owner/manager

Rejuvenate Skin & Body Clinic

Flourish Training Institute

Aurora Enterprise

rejuvenate@hotmail.com

www.rejuvenateyourbody.co.uk

About The Author

The inspiration for this book came from watching The Wolf Of Wall Street for the second time and immediately getting five powerful business principles. I then stayed up until 2am completing eight more. I delivered a presentation on it at Speakup Birmingham (See YouTube) and the interest from the audience made me want to explore the idea more.

https://www.facebook.com/groups/917756494926731/

This book was then written during the following week!

I am a certified Life/ success Coach with GO MAD
https://www.gomadthinking.com/

and I completed a business course with The Aston School of Social Entrepreneurs in 2006. I ran a course to help unemployed participants turn their hobbies into business which was funded by The European Social.

I understand people in business are busy, creative and determined to be successful. This book is for all of you.

These 365 principles are a brief reminder to help, support and encourage you on your path to success. It is deliberately short and sweet as I'm sure you know much of this already. Feel free to refer to the films and make notes at the back to record any additional insights you find.

https://www.solihullwellbeingclinic.com/?dti=1154707704616911&fref=g

www.browncherubsholistictherapies.com

Contents Page

1. The Wolf of Wall Street pg7
2. The Incredibles pg9
3. The Pursuit of Happyness pg11
4. Moana pg13
5. Hidden Figures pg15
6. The Amazing Spider Man pg17
7. Erin Brockovich pg19
8. The Croods pg21
9. 12 Years A Slave pg23
10. Iron Man pg25
11. Titanic pg27
12. Zootropolis pg29
13. 8 Mile pg31
14. Brave pg33
15. The Theory of Everything pg35
16. Sing pg37
17. The Imitation Game pg39
18. Boss Baby pg41
19. A Beautiful Mind pg43
20. 50 Shades Of Grey .... pg 45

17 business principles from The Wolf of Wall Street (Based on fact)

1. Having an addiction is not a barrier to success.
2. Selling – It's about the customer not the product or the seller. Why do they need the product? Why should they trust you?
3. Learn the formula from the best guide you can find in that field. Follow the formula with no exception.
4. Be yourself no matter who you are talking to, be your authentic self. Love you or hate you people will respect you.
5. Stick to your morals and beliefs. Let that be your sign posts. Good or bad, if it sits well with you, do it! If it doesn't don't!
6. Know when enough is enough. Set your goal, recognise when you have reached it and be satisfied.
7. Treat everyone with respect especially those that love you.
8. Tell a story. Paint a picture. Make them feel it.
9. Have fun. Enjoy the ride.
10. Take heed of sound advice.
11. Don't spend more than you make.
12. Pay what you owe.
13. Take a team with you. Think abundance, not scarcity.
14. Be driven by your need to improve your lifestyle.
15. If you are in debt – Pick up the phone. Take action.
16. March to the beat of your drum.
17. Be determined. DO NOT STOP UNTIL YOU GET WHAT YOU WANT!

17 Business Principles From The Incredibles

(Fiction)

18. Being married is not a barrier to success.
19. Everyone is Incredible.
20. Accept your strengths and weaknesses.
21. Never look back. It distracts you from the now.
22. Recognise the abilities of all those around you.
23. Trust your partner with the truth.
24. Hiding truths from your partner that affect them personally, can hurt them if they find out later on.
25. You cannot escape age and time.
26. Plan your exit strategy. Nothing lasts forever.
27. Combining all strengths together can compensate for all weaknesses.
28. Afford your loved ones some credit. They may be stronger than you think.
29. You may be the bread winner but everyone has a role to play in a family and all roles are equally important.
30. Partner up with people who lift you up not bring you down.
31. Surround yourself with people who can help you get where you need to go.
32. Ensure someone always knows where you are.
33. Research people you are going to do business with.
34. Be vulnerable but don't be weak.
35. Dress fit for purpose.

19 Business Principles From The Pursuit of Happyness (Based on Fact)

36. Your current financial situation is not a barrier to success.
37. Complete the Rubik's Cube.
38. Your children are your motivation not a hindrance.
39. Don't let anyone tell you what you can't achieve.
40. If others leave your table, stay, because it's your table.
41. You will experience 'good luck' and you will experience 'bad luck'. There is always both!
42. Treat yourself and others once in a while.
43. Finish whatever you have started. Focus on why you started it in the first place.
44. If you have invested money in something, ensure you get some return on that investment.
45. Show people what you can do. It's not arrogance it's confidence. People trust people who can demonstrate the skills to do the job. Blow your own trumpet.
46. If you don't know something yet, find out!
47. Be honest. Don't make excuse.
48. Find out who the person is at the top of that field. Strive to speak to them.
49. Have grace under pressure.
50. Master your craft. Do it better. Do it faster.
51. Go the extra mile.
52. Be likeable.
53. Recognise happiness in others and in yourself. That is what you want, not money.
54. Before you speak to anyone, smile.

19 Business Principles From
Moana
(Fiction)

55. Your gender is not a barrier to success.
56. Believe in who you are.
57. Follow your dream no matter where it takes you.
58. You only need one person to support you on your way.
59. Don't live your life through other people's fears and anxieties.
60. Just because others failed doesn't mean that you will.
61. Learn about your ancestors and honour them.
62. Practice your pitch. Say it with passion.
63. Learn the skills you need.
64. Go alone if you have to. You can pick up others on the way.
65. We all have our magic powers. (Skills and talents)
66. Persuade others to help you.
67. Face your challenges head on.
68. Try to understand your enemies. Once you understand, you can begin to overstand.
69. You have been chosen to walk the path of your life and your destiny awaits you at the end.
70. Decisions you make affects others and our planet.
71. Your loved ones are relying on you to achieve your goal.
72. Rest if you need to, but do not stop.
73. When you doubt your journey seek council only from those who really know you and care about you.

17 Business Principles From Hidden Figure (Based on Fact)

74. Your race is not a barrier to success.
75. You don't have to choose between being successful and having a relationship. You can have both.
76. Know your worth.
77. Think outside the box.
78. Stand up for yourself.
79. Stand up for others.
80. When you know you are right, speak your truth, even if your voice shakes.
81. You cannot expect everyone in your field to like you, but you can expect everyone in your field to respect you.
82. Lead from the front.
83. Do not be intimidated by those in higher posts than you.
84. With all due respect you can disagree with the current norm.
85. Being the first person to achieve something is AWESOME and well worth striving for.
86. 'Impossible' can also be 'I'm possible'. It's all just a matter of perspective.
87. No matter how you feel. Show up.
88. Don't let your emotions control your ability to perform.
89. Prove the nay-sayers wrong.
90. Dress for success.

16 Business Principles From
The Amazing Spider Man
(Fiction)

91. Being a 'looked after child' is not a barrier to success.
92. As long as somebody loves and cares about you, you will be ok. It doesn't have to be your real parents. (Mentee)
93. Every cloud has a silver lining if you choose to hold your head up and look for it.
94. People die. Be sad but don't let your sadness consume you.
95. You can study while you work.
96. Explore your skills, abilities and talents.
97. Stretch yourself.
98. It's ok to be rejected. You won't be everyone's cup of tea.
99. Do things which will make your loved ones proud of you.
100. Don't do things that would make your loved ones ashamed of you.
101. Do what you can to protect everything you care about.
102. Everyone doesn't have to know everything you do.
103. Stay humble.
104. Expect to have to make difficult decisions.
105. Accept the cards you are dealt. Hold on to your ace card. Play your best possible hand.
106. Be a high flyer.

22 Business Principles From Erin Brockovich (Based on fact)

107. Being a single parent is not a barrier to success.
108. Trust your instincts.
109. Go for every opportunity.
110. Focus on all your strengths.
111. Have your own style.
112. Be classy, not sassy.
113. Being a people person is a quality not everyone possesses.
114. If you can't get through on the phone, walk through the door.
115. Every life experience is an experience of life.
116. Accept any help and support which is genuine and sincere.
117. Where ever possible, cut out the middle man.
118. Be punctual.
119. Flattery can get you somewhere.
120. Your past does not define your future.
121. If you can do things other can't do... negotiate!
122. Once your clients trust you, treat them like friends.
123. Occasionally, do something just for the principle.
124. Don't assume everyone has the same moral code as you.
125. Stand and deliver. Stand by your word. Always deliver.
126. Know your stuff.
127. Pay attention to details.
128. Let people finish what they are saying. Don't interrupt.

17 Business Principles From
The Croods
(Fiction)

129. The time you live in is not a barrier to success.
130. Family first.
131. The needs of your family will change constantly be flexible.
132. Don't project your fears and anxieties on to your family or staff.
133. Not everyone is like you.
134. Appreciate the strengths and weaknesses of others.
135. Different generations have different ideas to you, not better or worse, just different.
136. Make the whole family a part of your goal so they feel that they are included in some way.
137. Embrace new ideas from others.
138. Create new ideas of your own.
139. Allow your circle to grow.
140. It isn't survival of the fittest; it's survival of those who can adapt to change.
141. Just because something was always done a certain way, doesn't mean that's the only way it can be done.
142. You can still be in charge, but let others lead.
143. Maximise all of the resources in your environment.
144. Get your inspiration from everywhere and everything.
145. Step out of your comfort zone. That is where the magic happens.

18 Business Principles From
12 Years A Slave
(Based on fact)

146. Your current situation is not a barrier to success.
147. Never forget who you are.
148. Even when you are apart, your loved ones are with you.
149. No matter how far you go, remember where you started.
150. Don't allow hard times to break your spirit.
151. Struggles can be used to develop your mental capacity.
152. Always develop your physical, mental and spiritual muscles.
153. Be comfortable at any table you accept the invitation to.
154. Stay alert.
155. Never compromise your core values.
156. Everything can change in just one day.
157. Rise above your prejudices – not everyone from one social group is the same.
158. Be compassionate, not everyone grieves like you do.
159. When times are hard, do what you do best.
160. Release your negative past experiences. Let them go, in order to embrace your positive future experiences.
161. No matter your circumstance, maintain your integrity, dignity and reputation. You never know who is watching.
162. If you witness injustice and can't speak up then, doesn't mean you can't speak up later.
163. Pay it forward. Give others the same break someone gave you.
164. Write your memoires. Share your journey. Be an inspiration for others.

18 Business Principles From
Iron Man
(Fiction)

165. Your past dealings are not a barrier to success.
166. Declare who you are! I am...!
167. You don't have to continue to do what you've always done.
168. Your intellectual property is valuable stuff. Protect it.
169. If you want to continue the family business you don't have to continue the family way.
170. You can make something out of anything.
171. Use technology. Don't let technology use you.
172. You can't have one foot on both sides of the fence.
173. Putting on armour doesn't make you brave; you have to be brave to put on armour.
174. Mind your business.
175. Don't pay people to do things you can do yourself.
176. Work smarter, not harder.
177. Don't be afraid to change direction. The view can look different from the top.
178. Tow the line between confidence and arrogance.
179. No one likes a know it all. Know more than you say.
180. What people think of you is none of your business.
181. Invest in you.
182. Others can try to copy your ideas, but they will never see your vision. (S. S. Brown)

21 Business Principles From

Titanic
(Based on fact)

183. The size of your dream is not a barrier to success.
184. The sky is not the limit. Your imagination is.
185. Dream as big as you dare.
186. Build it big. Build it safe.
187. Take all of the necessary precautions.
188. Risk assess all eventualities.
189. Get the best advice you can afford. If it makes sense, use it.
190. Anything made by man can be undone.
191. Understand the mechanics of your craft.
192. Never cut corners.
193. Pay attention to detail. Or pay someone else to.
194. Check, double check and check again.
195. You can plan a picnic, but you can't predict the weather.
196. If plan 'A' doesn't work, the alphabet has other letters.
197. Give people what they pay for.
198. Your failings should not cost others dearly.
199. Make the headlines for all the right reasons.
200. Take full responsibility for everything that happens.
201. Have a range of prices for your products or services so they are accessible to all.
202. Have a premium package for the elite.
203. Love is a very powerful emotion. Love what you do.

19 Business Principles From Zootropolis
(Fiction)

204. Your size is not a barrier to success.
205. If you believe you can make a change, make it.
206. You don't need permission to be who you are.
207. Who you are isn't just about your genetics.
208. Those who can't make a difference won't believe that you can.
209. Treat everyone the same.
210. Treat others as you expect to be treated.
211. Your loved ones have every right to be scared of the risks you chose to make. They have a vested interest in your life.
212. Reassure your loved ones that you have done a risk assessment.
213. Be willing to start from the bottom and work your way up to the top.
214. Expect to make mistakes.
215. A mistake is not the end of the journey.
216. You can give people a second chance. Forgive but don't forget.
217. The less others expect from you, the more you can surprise them.
218. Try things that people would never think that 'someone like you' would dare to do.
219. Sometimes your destiny is closely linked to the destiny of others. If you do it for you, you do it for them too.
220. Those with the most to say aren't always the ones you should be listening to.
221. If you can't reach. Elevate yourself and jump.
222. Challenge the social system.

19 Business Principles From 8 Mile
(Based on fact)

223. Your social class is not a barrier to success.
224. You are not the difficult circumstances which may surround you.
225. It is easier to help folks out of their pit from above them, rather than beside them.
226. When your passion is all you can think about, do it. Seize the moment.
227. Let your passion become your purpose.
228. One of your biggest barriers is your own ego.
229. You are only accountable for your own behaviour, not that of others.
230. Your friends do not have to be the same as you.
231. Know yourself, control yourself, be yourself.
232. Be able to laugh at yourself.
233. Turn pain into power.
234. Live it, breathe it, be it.
235. Walk the walk and talk the talk.
236. If you got it, flaunt it.
237. Give the people what they want.
238. Your personal story is your USP.
239. Research those that threaten you.
240. Make the most of the people you know in useful positions. They will be flattered.
241. Write it down as soon as you think it. Even on your hand.

17 Business Principles From
Brave
(Fiction)

242. Your hair colour or style is not a barrier to success.
243. Face your fear and confront your demons.
244. Traditions can be changed.
245. If you have the power to challenge current beliefs, use it.
246. Stand up for what is right, even if you have to stand alone.
247. Be careful what you wish for.
248. Don't buy products from those you don't know or trust.
249. Be sure things you buy come with insurance or warranty.
250. Don't accept second best.
251. Find time to have fun.
252. Be strong enough to defend yourself and your business.
253. Nobody knows everything. But everybody knows something.
254. Whenever you think about quitting, remember who is watching.
255. You are a role model, whether you chose to be or not.
256. Bringing people together is more powerful than driving people apart.
257. Put right things that you get wrong.
258. Tell those you love, that you love them.

19 Business Principles From
The Theory Of Everything
(Based on Fact)

259. Disabilities are not a barrier to success.
260. Find something to challenge you every day
261. Don't leave important things until the last minute.
262. When you have a big problem, look at the stars. It helps put things into perspective.
263. You don't have to agree on everything to be friends.
264. Focus on all the things you can do rather than the things you can't do.
265. It's not about the person in the fight; it's about the fight in the person.
266. If you can't fly, run. If you can't run, walk. If you can't walk, crawl. (Martin Luther King Jr.) As long as you are moving forward, you are making progress.
267. Treat everyone equally. Isolation hurts.
268. Share your ideas with who ever will listen.
269. Defy all expectations.
270. Retain a sense of humour.
271. Share the burdens you carry with those who love you.
272. Occasionally, enjoy the finer things in life.
273. There are many things in life money can't buy.
274. Your health is your wealth.
275. Try new solutions to problems. If there aren't any, invent one.
276. Work with those who speak your language.
277. No matter how bad life seems, there is always something you can succeed at. (Professor Stephen Hawking)

20 Business Principles From
Sing
(Fiction)

278. Having other responsibilities is not a barrier to success.
279. Walk away from toxic relationships: business or personal.
280. You don't have to be a part of the family business just because you're a part of the family.
281. Overcome your limitations to embrace your dream.
282. If you need an investor, choose carefully.
283. The show must go on.
284. Pair staff up to work together if someone is struggle alone.
285. Employ those who can do the job.
286. Lots can be learned from a mistake. Take a look. Don't just disregard them.
287. Competition is good, collaboration is better, teamwork is best.
288. Those that cannot commit fully can still contribute.
289. Sing from the same sheet but a choir appreciates various tones.
290. Don't judge people by their appearance or circumstances.
291. Be loyal to loyal staff.
292. Pay your bills on time.
293. Keep up with maintenance.
294. If you offer bonuses or rewards, have them and give them.
295. Some people just need an opportunity to shine.
296. If people have genuine talent, praise them, celebrate it.
297. Be inclusive and appreciate diversity.

18 Business Principles From
The Imitation Game
(Based on fact)

298. Your sexuality is not a barrier to success.
299. Don't be intimidated by those in authority.
300. Don't just do things you can do, do things you can't do.
301. See your challenges as play. Play is fun.
302. Be a team player.
303. Communicate clearly. Mean what you say and say what you mean.
304. Everything created by people, begins with an idea.
305. Use the best possible team and resources available.
306. "It's the people that nobody images anything from, that do the things people can't imagine." (The Imitation Game)
307. People may fear your uniqueness, that's their problem.
308. If you get blocked, speak to the person at the top.
309. Sometimes you have to show them your vision if they can't see it.
310. Get rid of the dead wood. It's business. It's not personal.
311. People will help you, if they like you.
312. Stand firm in what and who you believe in.
313. The Universe it always talking to you, if you choose to listen.
314. When things don't work it doesn't mean they are broken.
315. To get the right answers, you need to ask the right questions.

15 Business Principles From
Boss Baby
(Fiction)

316. Your current level of education is not a barrier to success.
317. Be willing to learn new things.
318. Those younger than you can teach you things too.
319. Finding common goals makes partnerships rather than competitors.
320. Think abundance not scarcity. There is enough of everything, for everyone.
321. Try not to casually reject others. This can create enemies.
322. Share your vision with your team.
323. Use memos.
324. If others threaten your position, consider if that is still the position for you.
325. Treat everyone equally to reduce resentment.
326. People are always watching how you treat others, even when you don't realise it.
327. Use your imagination. It is a powerful tool.
328. Question where things come from.
329. Recognise and be honest to your own feelings.
330. Make decisions based on the greater good of all, not just your own insecurities and ego.

19 Business Principles From
A Beautiful Mind
(Based on Fact)

331. Mental health conditions are not a barrier to success.
332. Consider your role model. Strive to have similar qualities.
333. Be around like minded people.
334. Don't be easily distracted.
335. Work when you are at work.
336. If you have specialist knowledge – publish.
337. Occasionally accept a challenge.
338. It's not enough to know, you have to do.
339. When it stops being fun, it's time to stop.
340. Do what's best for your business and for yourself.
341. Understand the philosophy of your field.
342. You don't have to win them all. Others want to win too.
343. Your way is not the only way.
344. Some will understand you, others won't. That's ok.
345. If you listen to what people say, you will know what they want.
346. There are many other things in life, besides your work.
347. Know your triggers and control them. Everyone has triggers.
348. Get the recognition you deserve for your work.
349. The very nature of being brilliant is seeing things others don't see.

16 Business Principles From 50 Shades Of Grey (Fiction)

350. Having suffered abuse is not a barrier to success.
351. A negative experience can become a powerful motivation.
352. Free yourself from negative past experiences that limit you now.
353. Try to understand your behaviours and your beliefs.
354. Allow those you love and trust to help you through difficult situations.
355. It can be lonely at the top, but you are never alone.
356. Be guarded but trust your chosen few.
357. Be generous.
358. Consider becoming a philanthropist.
359. Do people know what you do? Contact the media.
360. Spend time with your loved ones when you can.
361. You don't need to control people to be in control.
362. You don't have to agree with others to respect them.
363. Bounce your ideas off a team. If you don't have a team invest in a Life Coach.
364. Some people need you more than they need your money.
365. No matter your past or present circumstances, if you have earned your success, you deserve it!

Your Notes and Insights

Appendices:

Research Film Information Taken from:

https://en.wikipedia.org

11ᵗʰ September 2017

The Wolf of Wall Street

The Wolf of Wall Street

Theatrical release poster

Directed by	Martin Scorsese
Produced by	Martin Scorsese Leonardo DiCaprio Riza Aziz Joey McFarland Emma Tillinger Koskoff
Screenplay by	Terence Winter

Based on	*The Wolf of Wall Street* by Jordan Belfort
Starring	Leonardo DiCaprio Jonah Hill Margot Robbie Matthew McConaughey Kyle Chandler Rob Reiner Jon Bernthal Jon Favreau Jean Dujardin
Cinematography	Rodrigo Prieto
Edited by	Thelma Schoonmaker
Production companies	Red Granite Pictures Appian Way Productions Sikelia Productions EMJAG Productions
Distributed by	Paramount Pictures
Release date	December 17, 2013 (Ziegfeld Theatre) December 25, 2013 (United States)
Running time	179 minutes [1]
Country	United States
Language	English
Budget	$100 million [2][3]
Box office	$392 million [2]

The Incredibles

The Incredibles

Theatrical release poster

Directed by	Brad Bird
Produced by	John Walker
Written by	Brad Bird
Starring	Craig T. Nelson Holly Hunter Sarah Vowell Spencer Fox Jason Lee Samuel L. Jackson Elizabeth Peña
Music by	Michael Giacchino
Cinematography	Andrew Jimenez Patrick Lin Janet Lucroy

Edited by	Stephen Schaffer
Production company	Walt Disney Pictures Pixar Animation Studios
Distributed by	Buena Vista Pictures
Release date	October 27, 2004 (London Film Festival) November 5, 2004 (United States)
Running time	115 minutes[1]
Country	United States
Language	English
Budget	$92 million
Box office	$633 million[2]

The Pursuit of Happyness

The Pursuit of Happyness

Theatrical release poster

Directed by	Gabriele Muccino
Produced by	Will Smith Todd Black Jason Blumenthal James Lassiter Steve Tisch
Written by	Steven Conrad
Based on	*The Pursuit of Happiness* by Chris Gardner
Starring	Will Smith Thandie Newton Jaden Smith
Music by	Andrea Guerra
Cinematography	Phedon Papamichael

Edited by	Hughes Winborne
Production company	Relativity Media Overbrook Entertainment Escape Artists
Distributed by	Columbia Pictures (Sony Pictures Releasing)
Release date	December 15, 2006
Running time	117 minutes
Country	United States
Language	English
Budget	$55 million[1]
Box office	$307.1 million[1]

Moana

Moana

Theatrical release poster

Directed by	Ron Clements John Musker
Produced by	Osnat Shurer
Screenplay by	Jared Bush
Story by	Ron Clements John Musker Chris Williams Don Hall Pamela Ribon Aaron Kandell Jordan Kandell
Starring	Auli'i Cravalho Dwayne Johnson Rachel House Temuera Morrison Jemaine Clement Nicole Scherzinger Alan Tudyk

Music by	Mark Mancina Lin-Manuel Miranda (songs) Opetaia Foa'i (songs)
Edited by	Jeff Draheim
Production companies	Walt Disney Pictures Walt Disney Animation Studios
Distributed by	Walt Disney Studios Motion Pictures
Release date	November 14, 2016 (AFI Fest) November 23, 2016 (United States)
Running time	107 minutes
Country	United States
Language	English
Budget	$150 million[1][2][3]
Box office	$643 million[4]

Hidden Figures

Hidden Figures

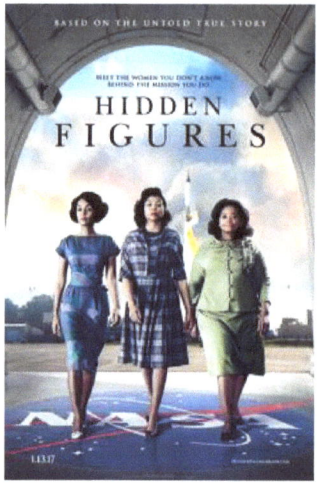

Theatrical release poster

Directed by	Theodore Melfi
Produced by	Donna Gigliotti Peter Chernin Jenno Topping Pharrell Williams Theodore Melfi
Screenplay by	Allison Schroeder Theodore Melfi
Based on	*Hidden Figures* by Margot Lee Shetterly
Starring	Taraji P. Henson Octavia Spencer Janelle Monáe Kevin Costner Kirsten Dunst Jim Parsons
Music by	Hans Zimmer

	Pharrell Williams Benjamin Wallfisch
Cinematography	Mandy Walker
Edited by	Peter Teschner
Production company	Fox 2000 Pictures Chernin Entertainment Levantine Films
Distributed by	20th Century Fox
Release date	December 10, 2016 (SVA Theatre) December 25, 2016 (United States)
Running time	127 minutes[1]
Country	United States
Language	English
Budget	$25 million[2][3]
Box office	$231.3 million[2]

The Amazing Spider Man

The Amazing Spider-Man

Theatrical release poster

Directed by	Marc Webb
Produced by	Avi Arad Matt Tolmach Laura Ziskin
Screenplay by	James Vanderbilt Alvin Sargent Steve Kloves
Story by	James Vanderbilt
Based on	*The Amazing Spider-Man* by Stan Lee Steve Ditko
Starring	Andrew Garfield Emma Stone Rhys Ifans Denis Leary Campbell Scott

	Irrfan Khan Martin Sheen Sally Field
Music by	James Horner
Cinematography	John Schwartzman
Edited by	Alan Edward Bell Michael McCusker Pietro Scalia
Production company	Marvel Entertainment[1] Laura Ziskin Productions Arad Productions, Inc. Matt Tolmach Productions
Distributed by	Columbia Pictures
Release date	June 30, 2012 (Tokyo) July 3, 2012 (United States)
Running time	136 minutes[2]
Country	United States
Language	English
Budget	$200–230 million[1]
Box office	$757.9 million[3]

Erin Brockovich

\br\br *Erin Brockovich* 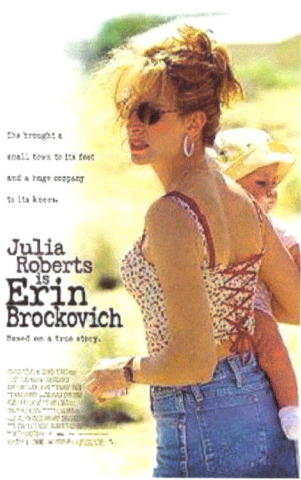 Theatrical release poster	
Directed by	Steven Soderbergh
Produced by	Danny DeVito Michael Shamberg Stacey Sher
Written by	Susannah Grant
Starring	Julia Roberts Albert Finney Aaron Eckhart
Music by	Thomas Newman
Cinematography	Ed Lachman
Edited by	Anne V. Coates
Production company	Jersey Films

Distributed by	Universal Pictures (USA & Canada) Columbia Pictures (International)
Release date	March 17, 2000
Running time	130 minutes
Country	United States
Language	English
Budget	$52 million
Box office	$256.3 million

The Croods

The Croods

Theatrical release poster

Directed by	Kirk DeMicco Chris Sanders
Produced by	Kristine Belson Jane Hartwell
Screenplay by	Kirk DeMicco Chris Sanders
Story by	John Cleese[1] Kirk DeMicco Chris Sanders
Starring	Nicolas Cage Emma Stone Ryan Reynolds Catherine Keener Clark Duke Cloris Leachman

Music by	Alan Silvestri[2]
Edited by	Eric Dapkewicz Darren T. Holmes
Production company	DreamWorks Animation
Distributed by	20th Century Fox
Release date	February 15, 2013 (Berlin) March 22, 2013 (United States)
Running time	98 minutes[3]
Country	United States
Language	English
Budget	$135 million[4]
Box office	$587.2 million[4]

12 Years A Slave

12 Years a Slave

Theatrical release poster

Directed by	Steve McQueen
Produced by	Brad Pitt Dede Gardner Jeremy Kleiner Bill Pohlad Steve McQueen Arnon Milchan Anthony Katagas
Screenplay by	John Ridley
Based on	*Twelve Years a Slave* by Solomon Northup
Starring	Chiwetel Ejiofor Michael Fassbender Benedict Cumberbatch Paul Dano Paul Giamatti Lupita Nyong'o

	Sarah Paulson Brad Pitt Alfre Woodard
Music by	Hans Zimmer
Cinematography	Sean Bobbitt
Edited by	Joe Walker
Production companies	Summit Entertainment Regency Enterprises River Road Entertainment Plan B Entertainment New Regency Productions Film4 Productions
Distributed by	Fox Searchlight Pictures (United States) Lionsgate (International)
Release date	August 30, 2013 (Telluride Film Festival) November 8, 2013 (United States) January 10, 2014 (United Kingdom)
Running time	134 minutes[1]
Country	United States United Kingdom
Language	English
Budget	$17.1 million[2]
Box office	$187.7 million[3]

Iron Man

Iron Man

Theatrical release poster

Directed by	Jon Favreau
Produced by	Avi Arad Kevin Feige
Screenplay by	Mark Fergus Hawk Ostby Art Marcum Matt Holloway
Based on	Iron Man by Stan Lee Larry Lieber Don Heck Jack Kirby
Starring	Robert Downey Jr. Terrence Howard Jeff Bridges Shaun Toub Gwyneth Paltrow

Music by	Ramin Djawadi
Cinematography	Matthew Libatique
Edited by	Dan Lebental
Production company	Marvel Studios Fairview Entertainment
Distributed by	Paramount Pictures[1]
Release date	April 14, 2008 (Sydney premiere) May 2, 2008 (United States)
Running time	126 minutes[1]
Country	United States
Language	English
Budget	$140 million[2]
Box office	$585.2 million[2]

Titanic

Titanic

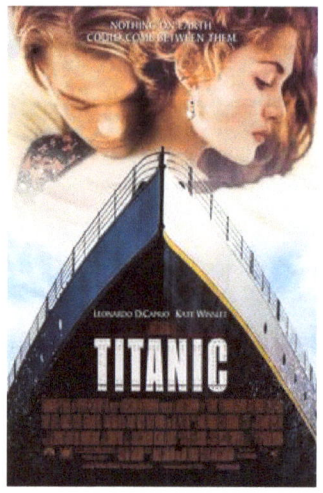

Theatrical release poster

Directed by	James Cameron
Produced by	James Cameron Jon Landau
Written by	James Cameron
Starring	Leonardo DiCaprio Kate Winslet Billy Zane Kathy Bates Frances Fisher Bernard Hill Jonathan Hyde Danny Nucci David Warner Bill Paxton
Music by	James Horner
Cinematography	Russell Carpenter

Edited by	Conrad Buff James Cameron Richard A. Harris
Production company	Paramount Pictures[1] 20th Century Fox[1] Lightstorm Entertainment[1]
Distributed by	Paramount Pictures (North America) 20th Century Fox (International)
Release date	November 1, 1997 (Tokyo) December 19, 1997 (United States)
Running time	195 minutes[2]
Country	United States
Language	English
Budget	$200 million[3][4][5]
Box office	$2.187 billion[6]

Zootropolis

Zootopia

Theatrical release poster

Directed by	Byron Howard Rich Moore
Produced by	Clark Spencer
Screenplay by	Jared Bush Phil Johnston[1]
Story by	Byron Howard Rich Moore Jared Bush Jim Reardon Josie Trinidad Phil Johnston Jennifer Lee
Starring	Ginnifer Goodwin Jason Bateman Idris Elba Jenny Slate Nate Torrence Bonnie Hunt Don Lake

	Tommy Chong J. K. Simmons Octavia Spencer Alan Tudyk Shakira
Music by	Michael Giacchino
Cinematography	Nathan Warner Brian Leach
Edited by	Fabienne Rawley Jeremy Milton
Production company	Walt Disney Pictures Walt Disney Animation Studios
Distributed by	Walt Disney Studios Motion Pictures
Release date	February 10, 2016 (Belgium) March 4, 2016 (United States)
Running time	108 minutes[2][3]
Country	United States
Language	English
Budget	$150 million[4]
Box office	$1.024 billion[5]

8 Mile

8 Mile

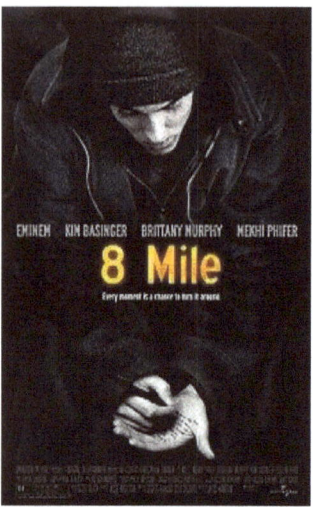

Theatrical release poster

Directed by	Curtis Hanson
Produced by	Curtis Hanson Brian Grazer Jimmy Iovine
Written by	Scott Silver
Starring	Eminem Kim Basinger Brittany Murphy Mekhi Phifer
Cinematography	Rodrigo Prieto
Edited by	Jay Rabinowitz

Production company	Imagine Entertainment
Distributed by	Universal Pictures
Release date	November 8, 2002
Running time	110 minutes[1]
Country	United States
Language	English
Budget	$41 million[2]
Box office	$242.9 million[2]

Brave

Brave

Theatrical release poster

Directed by	Mark Andrews Brenda Chapman
Produced by	Katherine Sarafian
Screenplay by	Mark Andrews Steve Purcell Brenda Chapman Irene Mecchi
Story by	Brenda Chapman
Starring	Kelly Macdonald Billy Connolly Emma Thompson Julie Walters Robbie Coltrane Kevin McKidd Craig Ferguson

Music by	Patrick Doyle
Cinematography	Robert Anderson Danielle Feinberg
Edited by	Nicholas C. Smith
Production company	Walt Disney Pictures Pixar Animation Studios
Distributed by	Walt Disney Studios Motion Pictures
Release date	June 10, 2012 (SIFF) June 22, 2012 (United States)
Running time	94 minutes[1]
Country	United States
Language	English
Budget	$185 million[2]
Box office	$540.4 million[3]

The Theory of Everything

The Theory of Everything

UK release banner

Directed by	James Marsh
Produced by	Tim Bevan Eric Fellner Lisa Bruce Anthony McCarten
Screenplay by	Anthony McCarten
Based on	*Travelling to Infinity: My Life with Stephen* by Jane Wilde Hawking
Starring	Eddie Redmayne Felicity Jones Charlie Cox Emily Watson Simon McBurney David Thewlis
Music by	Jóhann Jóhannsson
Cinematography	Benoît Delhomme
Edited by	Jinx Godfrey
Production company	Working Title Films

Distributed by	Universal Pictures (UK & International) Focus Features (US)
Release date	7 September 2014 (TIFF) 1 January 2015 (United Kingdom)
Running time	123 minutes[1][2]
Country	United Kingdom
Language	English
Budget	$15 million[3]
Box office	$123.7 million[3]

Sing

Sing

Theatrical release poster

Directed by	Garth Jennings
Produced by	Chris Meledandri Janet Healy
Written by	Garth Jennings
Starring	Matthew McConaughey Reese Witherspoon Seth MacFarlane Scarlett Johansson John C. Reilly Taron Egerton Tori Kelly
Music by	Joby Talbot
Edited by	Gregory Perler[1]

Production company	Universal Pictures Illumination Entertainment
Distributed by	Universal Pictures
Release date	September 11, 2016 (TIFF) December 21, 2016 (United States)
Running time	108 minutes[1]
Country	United States
Language	English
Budget	$75 million[2]
Box office	$632.4 million[2]

The Imitation Game

The Imitation Game

British theatrical release poster

Directed by	Morten Tyldum
Produced by	Nora Grossman Ido Ostrowsky Teddy Schwarzman
Written by	Graham Moore
Based on	*Alan Turing: The Enigma* by Andrew Hodges
Starring	Benedict Cumberbatch Keira Knightley Matthew Goode Rory Kinnear Charles Dance Mark Strong
Music by	Alexandre Desplat

Cinematography	Óscar Faura
Edited by	William Goldenberg
Production companies	Black Bear Pictures Bristol Automotive
Distributed by	The Weinstein Company
Release date	August 29, 2014 (Telluride Film Festival) November 28, 2014 (United States)
Running time	114 minutes[1]
Country	United States[2][3]
Language	English
Budget	$14 million[4]
Box office	$233.6 million[5]

Boss Baby

The Boss Baby

Theatrical release poster

Directed by	Tom McGrath
Produced by	Ramsey Ann Naito
Screenplay by	Michael McCullers
Based on	*The Boss Baby* by Marla Frazee
Starring	Alec Baldwin Steve Buscemi Miles Bakshi Jimmy Kimmel Lisa Kudrow Tobey Maguire
Music by	Hans Zimmer Steve Mazzaro
Edited by	James Ryan

Production company	DreamWorks Animation
Distributed by	20th Century Fox
Release date	March 12, 2017 (Miami) March 31, 2017 (United States)
Running time	97 minutes[1]
Country	United States
Language	English
Budget	$125 million[2]
Box office	$498.8 million[3]

A Beautiful Mind

A Beautiful Mind

Theatrical release poster

Directed by	Ron Howard
Produced by	Brian Grazer Ron Howard
Screenplay by	Akiva Goldsman
Based on	*A Beautiful Mind* by Sylvia Nasar
Starring	Russell Crowe Ed Harris Jennifer Connelly Paul Bettany Adam Goldberg Judd Hirsch Josh Lucas Anthony Rapp Christopher Plummer
Music by	James Horner

Cinematography	Roger Deakins
Edited by	Daniel P. Hanley Mike Hill
Production company	Imagine Entertainment
Distributed by	Universal Pictures (North America) DreamWorks Pictures (International)
Release date	December 13, 2001 (Beverly Hills premiere) December 21, 2001 (United States)
Running time	135 minutes
Country	United States
Language	English
Budget	$58 million[1]
Box office	$313 million[1]

50 Shades Of Grey

Fifty Shades of Grey

Theatrical release poster

Directed by	Sam Taylor-Johnson
Produced by	Michael De Luca E. L. James Dana Brunetti
Screenplay by	Kelly Marcel
Based on	*Fifty Shades of Grey* by E. L. James
Starring	Dakota Johnson Jamie Dornan Jennifer Ehle Marcia Gay Harden
Music by	Danny Elfman
Cinematography	Seamus McGarvey

Edited by	Debra Neil-Fisher Anne V. Coates Lisa Gunning
Production companies	Michael De Luca Productions
Distributed by	Universal Pictures Focus Features
Release date	February 9, 2015 (Los Angeles) February 13, 2015 (United States)
Running time	128 minutes[1]
Country	United States
Language	English
Budget	$40 million[2]
Box office	$571 million[2]

www.browncherubsholistictherapies.com

See my range of books...

Mrs Myrah Duckworth(B.Ed)

Find me on:

 behappy.me quotes by Myrah Duckworth

 browncherub1

 Browncherub Publishing

 @BrownCherub1

 Myrah Duckworth

BROWN CHERUB

www.browncherubsholistictherapies.com

www.ingramcontent.com/pod-product-compliance
Lightning Source LLC
Chambersburg PA
CBHW051202220526
45473CB00003B/877